FUGUE BODY

Fugue Body

BRIDGET HUH

Signal EDITIONS

THE POETRY IMPRINT AT VÉHICULE PRESS

Published with the generous assistance of the Canada Council for the
Arts and the Canada Book Fund of the Department of
Canadian Heritage.

Canada Council   Conseil des arts
for the Arts   du Canada   Canadä

SIGNAL EDITIONS EDITOR: Michael Prior
Cover design by David Drummond
Photo of the author by Isabela Marino
Set in Minion and Filosofia by Simon Garamond
Printed by Livres Rapido Books

Copyright © Bridget Huh 2025
All rights reserved.

Dépôt légal, Library and Archives Canada and the
Bibliothèque national du Québec, first trimester 2025

Library and Archives Canada Cataloguing in Publication

Title: Fugue body / Bridget Huh.
Names: Huh, Bridget, author.
Identifiers: Canadiana (print) 2025011299X | Canadiana (ebook)
20250113023 | ISBN 9781550656763
(softcover) | ISBN 9781550656817 (EPUB)
Subjects: LCGFT: Poetry.
Classification: LCC PS8615.U3198 F84 2025 | DDC C811/.6—dc23

Published by Véhicule Press, Montréal, Québec, Canada
vehiculepress.com

Distribution in Canada by LitDistCo
litdistco.ca

Distribution in the U.S. by Independent Publishers Group
ipgbook.com

Printed in Canada on FSC certified paper.

CONTENTS

Emergency Orchestra 9
Fugue Body 10
I, the poet, the euphemist 24
Portrait of Soloist 28
From Which Time 29
Portrait of IIIIIIIII 34
Camera 36
Portrait of EEEEEEEEE 42
Portrait of Sibelius 43
Silence of Järvenpää 56
Touching the Verb 58
Sometimes I'm 61
Las Calles 63
Seascape Suite 79
Ode 83
Emergency Orchestra 85
Portrait of Accompanist 87
On Disappointments in Music 88
Aria 89
Yellow 90
Modality 91
Lyric You 93
Emergency Orchestra 94
Argument 95

NOTES 99
ACKNOWLEDGEMENTS 100

Emergency Orchestra

For what we call the present.

For the sake of future loss.

For what we hope will endure.

For the essential nature of a work.

For its body bound in time.

For the rhythm of a language.

For the glorification of singing.

Fugue Body

My body has always done what I have asked
of it. This is called communication, and also
confrontation. This is called being 19
& healthy.

Am I allowed to write about bodies? I think
so. I have one. It hangs onto me like
dampness, like deceit. It threatens

to slip right off and leave me
compact and helpless. Am I allowed? For me
the question is not who will stop

me but where I would find my entrance
into it. My body and I are too young
to realize our circle
that endless shape—

all things depart from
and arrive at the body. Enclosed
and enclosing. Such is the body. Yes, mine.

Enclosed until a white person holds it
in their enclosing eyes. I have white friends,
I do, I have friends

who wrap around me like a ring of yellowing teeth.
One is my roommate, White 1.

Another is a girl who wanted him, or his body.
She is White 2. This is how I tell them
apart.

White 1 tells me I am a stick figure. Weak
arms. White 2 asks, You're how many
pounds? I answer. One of them says

You weigh literally nothing.
I laugh and try to find my way

out of their stupid conversation.
Their reinventing of my body, the way
white people say things

you'd think their eyes were hands,
putting everything in its wrong place. The body
becomes bruised

in the body. Reinvention—how ingenious!
But it could not be any more obvious, Whites
1 & 2, what you want my image for, or

how you hide your own
behind it.

All of the people I know and love
have been carved into
still image

by white people. They have turned
their bodies into handprints.
The way language becomes

the body? The way
its lack leaves a body lost
& legless. English opened a hole

in the middle of my mother's chest
into which white people would stare
endlessly. This is not a poem about my mother

but it is about a body, and she did put me
in one. This is not a poem about my mother
but she gave me a body and in return asked me only

to line her mouth with knives. I did this
happily. I did this the only way I knew how.
What does this word mean? Say

breaths for me. Say *deaths*. The subtle break
between *ears* and *years*. Hold it
in the body, model the way it sits
on the tongue. This phrase. This cluster

of sound. In a way, my English became
hers. I call it my English not because it is mine
to command but because it commands

me, encloses the whole of my body
in its hands, which is to say I want to unskin
the outline of my body, peel it off with those bladed

eyes, each word a whetting, which is to say I live
in a body that English stole from my mother.
In a body that English has unbound

from *us*. *Me* or *you* or *them*,
a sentence of skin
closed all around each body—

To tell a body is to pull it out from a womb
-dark sea. To tell a body is to pull it
apart.

Once I realize
and eventually, I do,
how white people know

they can put their hands straight through
my body

I can never look at them
nor my body
the same way again.

There are always such thresholds. Again
I overcook the spinach. Thresholds against which

everything spills right through. The mouth
opens to give you everything and closes
around another name.

Things are better when I pretend
I've had no hand in making them.

In this city I make nothing
but noise. In this city a body is
tethered to a piano by arms

as tender and yielding as overcooked
spinach. I throw my wilting body
into Chopin's first Ballade, the G minor one

that everybody loves.
Schumann famously told Chopin that
it was his favourite of all his works.

Chopin replied, That pleases me
for it is also my favourite.
When I play it for the first time

in front of a real body
a professor I hope will teach me piano
he tells me my pedalling is muddling the notes.

He says, It's like a stain
blurring the music written on the page.
He is 71 years old, and correct.

Classically trained musicians have an unwavering
commitment to the score. But look: Chopin's body
is open, lets all the world

back into it and out. His heart pickles
in a jar. Who's to say, for certain,

how he would truly feel
about my body fumbling
his score, letting it slip

like a handful of light
through my glass fingers? Would his heart
deflate, tumble from its jar

at my touch, a torrent
of gray water, warping
the only part of his body

that still remains, still moves
the world? That voice singles out
in the manner

of a lighthouse beam
each individual
body.

His language is final.
The notated ever lyric, operatic.

Constrains multitudes, that certain body.
A certain body speaks
to and for all. But I? I know my body's constraints.

The problem with constraints is that once you feel
them you will never be able to free yourself
until your body

encloses them. Until the body
clings wetly over them, overcooked greens raised
on a fork, body pressed upwards by a core of bone,

until the body
encircles them as though
they began in there, as though

the body were a mother. Tell me:
Who would call this music? Even hope
is such a constraint.

When mothers tell you you've lost
weight what could they mean
but that you have realized a threshold and crossed

it, your body more tender, more pliant
for its loss? What did your escaped flesh
leave behind?

There were weeks in the city where I could not go
without at least a beer in the evenings.
Every evening.

Sometimes it was the bright noise
of Sainte-Catherine on a Saturday
night. It was all around me, a great throbbing
layering of pressure. Sometimes I just felt

alone in my new city
and pulled despair around my body in an embrace.
Sometimes I did not know what else to do
with myself.

White 1 says to me one day, Hey, you should date
White 2. She says she wants to date women.
I laugh. No, I say, I could never. And besides,

she doesn't date people of colour. Probably not
consciously. But she just doesn't.
White 1, who gets very defensive

whenever I open my raced
mouth, demands I explain.
But what is there to explain? What is the point
of putting language against it when you will never—

I explain anyway. Well, he says, she's from
a small town in Alberta. Only white people.
So? I said. So? If she is surrounded

by it she is forgiven the ignorance
her body allows her? Okay, I see
your point, he says. He pauses. Am I like that?

I consider lying. Yes,
I say. Obviously, I think
but do not say. He laughs.

He laughs loosely, his body shaking
like a fresh piece of wind. He laughs
and comes up against a body,

mine, shutting doors
to the cold, stiffening like a coat.

Yeah, he says, white people are weird about dating
people from other races. That, or they just
fetishize them. It's a Catch-22.

It should come as no surprise
that I haven't dated at all. This feels like a confession
in itself. A gaping admission. Like I have left my mouth

wide open, waiting for wet weather.
I want to blame it on circumstance. I want
to blame countries, one inescapable, the other

left behind in its solitary
ocean. I want to blame it on circumstance,
but it could entirely be

me, and my body, that circle of absence.
Whites 1 & 2 love to tell me that I am repressed.
It is their favourite joke to make at my expense.

I don't think I am, though. I do know desire.
I know it when it shows up, asking for
entrance, the beginning of the circle.

I know it is my enclosed body
that turns it away.

I rather like my hands.
But whenever I play the Ballade
I wish they were in love.

The 71-year-old piano teacher spent a long phrase
of time describing how the sound of the piano
is entirely handmade. How the sound exactly captures

the human touch, flings its question out towards
the listener. Waits for it to land. Waits
for its answer in the body.

Other hands have convinced me
that my body, the span of my hands
has no touch, no weight

to project. All things better, more beautiful
when I have no hand in making them.

The Ballade rings out like a mouth full
and wordless, each tooth a bell

naming itself, sitting in the lungs like
a fist of smoke, cages
& ribcages of howling for any body

to stay, just stay, the way it commands
bodies, the way it takes a body
with the momentum of an illness

—inevitable, it's written in the score
even as my body stands in the path
of its melody.

I return one night after only two drinks
to confrontation.

In the shower the body and I begin
to come undone.
The wall in front of me blurs

like a stain, a cascade of black notes
filling my blank eyes.
The shower suddenly quiets.

Has the water setting changed? A bar of silence.
A line.
It must be me, my body, someone says

to myself. Pedal muddling the sound of water
falling. My first thought is
No, I cannot shit in the shower no matter

how useless my body. I wonder if I can just
stay
in the shower till morning, by which time

I am sure my body will have returned
to me.
Somehow my body makes it out

of that box. I knock on White 1's door.
He helps me to the couch where I
collapse, foreign arms of water

filling with history. I leave my body
on it, carelessly, too afraid
that I will once again become lost

in the body, suppressed by a cage
of my own making.

What my body does
in my absence
is none of my concern.

My body finds its way back to Toronto
for the winter break. I don't know why
I expected that I would suddenly be happy,

that I could leave
the tender, helpless parts of myself
behind.

I don't know why I expected I'd ever be whole
now that I have split
my life between two cities.

I want to gather all of the people I love
and will love in my weeping branches
and crowd them into my body. I want to become
a vessel, or a mother.

Good technique, says the 71-year-old pianist,
is when the body gets out of the way. When the body
gets out of the way, the sound you imagine

can come out of here—he pats the box of the upright.
But look! All this time, I have kept his body
out of my way. The problem with him, and this is
the real problem,

is that I cannot cut into him, unpeel his body
to reveal his secret and innermost
white person thoughts. The problem

with him is that when I put him in my little house
of racelessness
which is where I live

with all of the white people
who have not held their bodies
over mine, or whose bodies
I would rather not think about

in relation to mine—he has not stayed put
where I left him. Nor can I quite force him
back in through the door. Bodies can be so

unwieldy. He would call this technical inability,
a lack of control. He would call this a body
in the way. I call it why is my raceless house

white? My raceless house holds its face up
on its sharp white walls of sharp white bricks.
Whiteness built my little house, and I chose to live
in it anyway.

Through my little window
streams my sharp asking eyes.
How dare he be exactly what he is,

which is a body
that will never answer the question
I have enclosed him in?

How dare he have
a real white body that is unaware
of the way I, in a fit of love,

tighten my hands
around it? I know no one
is perfect.

Some people are white.
Some people take you out
of your body

because that's love, or
desire. Or one is the other,
or the other's the other,

or the other is forgotten and
gone.

I think of it this way: my self, caught thick
in the box of my own body. Striking bars
of black rain. The body is always in the way.

One day I will find my way
around it, circling it
like a mirror. Enclosed
and enclosing.

I, the poet, the euphemist

1.

Some streets are softer
than sorry. Some streets so
sociable they stop you

all signs & slow speaking
your cheek pressed against
sidewalk. You soften to

sidewalk. You sigh, your mouth
full of feathers. What are you
doing down on the ground,

grandpa? Let me, speaking,
explain. Each cobbled gaze
chafes against you. Threads

of foreign ink unravel
from your flank. You'd think
holding your skin up before his eyes

would be enough to tell
your own story of surrender.
Don't think. What can you do

but listen to the boy
who put you there? Would he change
if I called him by some other

name? This boy blurs you
blurring before our eyes
shut. Can't bear to watch him

watching you.

2.

Some streets stop
just before sorry. Even I stop
just so. Down here, even the street

is an artist: its fingers drag lines
straight through your greying face
carving tire treads. Do you want me

to stop? I won't. I am here to tell you
what we have turned away from. I am here
to tell you you've gone, your fading face

not even feigning surprise. Like the policeman
who stood, who watched Vincent Chin
collide with a baseball bat and saw

a home run, full contact, he said,
full swing—I am here
to witness you. To put words

to your body. To put words
against the violence so that we can do better
violence. Watch me.

Some streets rise to greet you and ask
for a map of the yellow body. Ask to
plot it. Ask to plunder it. Me,

I'm here as a tour guide. Some streets
cross your body like a street. Some
streets paved for a white boy's

unyielding foot. All streets lead
to an amphitheatre—all streets lead to
spectacle. What are you

but a rain-dark stretch of asphalt.
Here we are, a uniform mass
of footprints. What do you mean

what am I doing here?
Didn't he put me here, too?
You don't reply.

On a street in New York
they open Noel Quintana's face like it was
a box. Peer inside, find nothing. The blade

so deep he couldn't speak. The passengers
sit. We watch. Each of us our own reasons
for violence and deserving. Each of us hoping

to hide in a crowd of us. Each turning away,
pretending he is an empty container
of rank subway air. Pretending we are that air.

3.

Look, you, the audience is white. The audience
speaks. Sometimes they applaud. I could go on
but won't. I could go on, but a deserted

amphitheatre. I could go on, but all these
streets lead you right to
me, my failed body. Let me sharpen

my blade of asking, grandpa.
What are you acting?
No, who for? To whom

does your performance belong?
How much more skin
before I reach your pulsing core?

You must forgive me if I write
too much about
or for white people.

You know it is only so I,
the poet, the euphemist
do not get mistaken

for myself.
It is only a matter of time
before a white boy's white gladiator

points his finger at me. Worse
before I point my finger at myself.
Here—this is art.

Take it.

Portrait of Soloist

Naturally I agreed to give
this concerto myself

I would like to extinguish
the sky I am about to do it

I allow myself great breathing
reverberations in every room

What they say about me
is mostly fiction

What they say about me makes me
neither big nor small

Doesn't everyone believe
they have something to say

Not me I speak
to contradict belief

A beautiful thing about speech
is that it ends

Let me go on
forever

From Which Time

Within the fold of a brief century
the time it took to perform the Sibelius
Violin Concerto spun outwards

from twenty-six or
twenty-eight minutes to
upwards of thirty-five.

It is hard to know how
much music fits inside
one minute or even

[where he pauses for a breath
opens the tunnel as if
coming to an exit]

how much might escape
from one inadequately
sealed. Heifetz who was

thought to have resurrected
the concerto recorded it
in 1935 with the London

Philharmonic under the
baton of Sir Thomas Beecham
its duration a cool

twenty-eight minutes and
fourteen seconds. That
sound was once ephemeral

[the Adagio tells me
how he must have looked
at her]

is hard to imagine harder
to believe. But listening
to Heifetz flicker

tone-worlds away from
here I am already
there—each note

introducing itself to me
not by name but by
the space it would have

[I hear his thoughts of
kissing her his fears he might
never see her again]

filled in his world as
though they could take
no form but these

sensible globes of immortal
ice which do not remain
so much as insist on their

being, and being,
and being. To say that
it is only a matter of time

[what if this is indeed
our last time
on this earth]

is to neglect the feeling
of an *allegro moderato*
or an *allegro ma non tanto*.

It was Beethoven who
made this distinction between
time which is in the body

and tempo which refers
to the soul. The first time
I heard this concerto I felt

[her brother said to him
don't look at my sister
like that]

as though I had lost
all sense of both.
I must have been

in The Box when he
appeared to me
timeless and glimmering

[like falling
in love at last
sight]

standing in the bend of
the grand piano holding
a bow but no violin.

His gaze had the weight
of an afternoon so densely
blue which pinned me

to the bench for thirty minutes
for eight whole hours
for no time at all

[no one will know how
I remember the weeping
of your violin]

To speak of gaining or
losing time is to use the
wrong language entirely

in such a work for
what time is taken
must always be given

[no one but those
who listen when I
conduct Sibelius]

back and so on. Which
raises the question:
from which time

have our extra minutes
been taken?

[who will wait
for their
return]

Portrait of IIIIIIIII

The first baton was none other than
a rib

Pried off the breastbone
as a face from the mirror

The rib and I are weaving
long threads of inward wind

Holding our breaths for the language
to describe what box contains us now

If I will get nowhere
listening only to the beautiful

What are the ugly sounds
let me make them for you

Blare of a sound too low for noise
Noise too noise for music

With what urgency
does the orchestra proceed

And is it prepared to face
the consequences

All of us out of time
All of us throats brimming

We are drifting off to get there
We are racing to get nowhere

Being unstrangled all together
is ugly in itself

Is there such an ugly
Is there such a sound

My unbruised neck says no
Wakes to an iron taste

Camera

In my school days I liked to be alone in The Box.
The Box was where I made my time beautiful.

It had two switches Light and Air.
I found it did not matter to music about Air.

I could not do anything about Light.
Without it the piano lost its deep edges.

And anyway light always finds a way in.
A box unfolds from many places.

Some have a pinhole.
Through which light rivers from eye to eye.

My housemate then had eyes only for his camera.
For he practiced the solitude of photography.

He felt it was his calling.
Calling or no he was never any good at listening.

He did not like to go outside to take pictures.
What was there to see inside you might ask.

A world asking to be composed.
Fistful of keys empty box of cigarettes.

Raw chicken breast greasing the counter.
Rich yellow of unwashed months.

A new bloom of black mold.
Beard hairs feebling in the kitchen sink.

One night I woke to the sound of a camera shutter closing.
I slept in a darkness that could only be achieved deliberately.

Hard lid on the night spill.
He knew this about me and yet.

And yet.
That is all I have to say about this night.

A photograph bears what I might call the imprint of a soul.
(In those days I was sure I had one.)

The gravest injury he had given me was this.
A shimmering chord axed at the root.

Not my soul in that image but his.
Streaming through the little crack in the door.

Pooling on the fresh film of my body.
(When I began to believe I did not.)

Only one thing to do after such an event.
I made myself aperture.

There was music firing at me from all sides.
A focused note made a striking image.

No other students ever sought out The Box.
I filled it with intention mine alone.

Of course I did not like that taste flooding my body.
But like it or not a life holds many remains.

Space was only one of them and yet it was all I had.
Space for what.

What came one evening I was alone.
With my Schubert I mean we liked our privacy.

Here was a precise and even knock on The Box.
The Box answered with a crack.

I ran to shut off Light and Air.
I fluttered to the door.

Through the pinhole I could see her violin.
Her first words to me were these.

I need accompanying.
Alone I hear you.

The Box closed all around us.
Lightless looking went both ways.

Sitting together in the dark we were like two hands.
What were we waiting for.

For *each* to swell with absence.
For *I* to unfold from its edges.

I dancing like a wick in candle flame.
I who became a tree who stayed the wind.

I is no way to live.
It is no way to want.

Sing me away from the world.
Sing me a way into *I*.

In the beginning there were these two Light and Air.
In the beginning not even *I* was.

She lifted the violin like a shaft of bright wind.
Unwound a voice like a stream of slow-melting tears.

Each note wore a backwards face.
Asked questions I could no longer answer.

Was it a dream.
Or did it only have that quality of dreams.

Convincing dreamers of something.
That for a long time they have already known.

As in the lays of winter cold and ancient rain.
Songs bottled by the bird that you once were.

The bow hung on the tip.
No room to breathe.

Could I see her body.
Or was the body in my image only mine.

The degree of personhood was mounting.
That is to say I was cut down the middle

I split on the shards of listening
Not a wound but a crack of an egg's shell

Out of which spills golden Light translucent Air
Not a wound but another way out of myself

Yes I will accompany you forever
As two parallel rivers seeking the same ocean

Did you want to know what I felt
I always dream of brides

Tucked under your arm the violin said nothing
I could still understand its soul

Animacy is a kind of gender
It is a matter of gradience

Who decided that more soul animates *I*
Than *it* which might bear the world

Certainly it had no say in the matter
It merely means matter

It lacks the rational soul of us
The falsehood

Like a photograph it is always invisible
It is not it that we see

What is it that we see
What is it that we crush with seeing

A photograph shatters   an object's animacy
One less piece   of soul inside

Perhaps it is this   felt absence
That which Barthes   called the *punctum*

If this moment   were a photograph
Afraid of crushing you   my gaze holds the violin

If it is   a fallen dream wife
It speaks   in the wide *I* of violin.

I takes   its time
It waits   for time's return

Portrait of EEEEEEEEE

Violin rehearses the gape of a sorrow.
Red memory of one two three four hammers.

Violin is sprouting her wildflower giggles.
Violin wraps a long neck around my wrist.

Violin's blue tremors wrack the sea.
Violin's sentences rise and fall like a wave.

Violin tires of swimming.
Violin is in her bare mind.

Let's sharpen Violin's strings.
Let's sharpen Violin's EEEEEEEEE

Violin has a daughter called.
Silence it is over now.

No a son he is called how.
Many claps amount to applause.

Violin cries herself to EEEEEEEEE
Branches grow over Violin's weeping.

Portrait of Sibelius

PROEM

As for tempo: what with time
has slackened to wandering.

My voice wanders
the empty picture frame—

[Where have you gone?
How long will my voice stand
in for your meaning?]

No, I do not know
if he will be in tomorrow.

Jean, what do you see?
Jean, you must answer me
one day with more than
your corpus of bewilderment.

Forget eyes now.
Forget all but

that which you ask
of no one but god.

I. ALLEGRO MODERATO

A prayer sul G to fill
the great hunger years.
Rain hunches over

the beetblight fields.
Father hunches over
the bedridden.

Father the bedridden
falls into flight!

What eye forgets
the furniture remembers.
Cigar smoke smell
rawing the inside out.

[Shall we beat
the early character
of his life

in two
or in four?]

In a little book
of animal pictures
one woodcock

rises out of white mist
suspended
at the edge of its
moment.

Many perch sink
back into silver
sleep

slow sheets seething
over them.

Uncountable southerly
winds race
up the shore

throwing
saltsea touches
into my hands.

Papa will you
never
come again

even if I
call
you
three or
five times?

∼

Mothers dream
of accidents.

Mothers
set trembling
questions free
in a boy's

burning body.
Janne, I had
that dream again—
Janne, have you had

that imminent break—
[His violin mustered
a fissure.]

O Maria
what did you

ask
of no one

but god?
What did you

wail at the pitch
of prayer

storming
striving

tender throat
towering atop

a column of thunder
utter
urgent
unknown—

Father could be asleep
in the drawing-room

fitting calmly in his
coffin.

Janne on the
hunting horn
toots a farewell:
Run away good reindeer!

Let us keep quiet
we who are hungry
we who are sick
we who are isolate houses.

∾

Thus the hired
fortepiano

becomes its own
square room.

Square piano
plucks snow
out of its flight
like a roof.

Square piano weaves
threads of icy light.

Janne is dressed
in these bright tones.

A major:
blue to bury bone
-weary barques.

C major:
red of rusty
railroad
rushing.

D major:
yearning
for yesterday's
yolk yellow.

F major:
grave
grieving green
ghostgrip.

Each note
a glittering glass ball!

Glass balls
slipped

from his five-year-old
fingers.
Aunt Julia with her
knitting needles—*rap, rap*.

How could a note
declare itself
in a mind
by anything but

its own name!
Those notes which
glaze light
in a colour!

Turtledove
croons blue
-grey *re*.

Woodpigeon
warble seeks
sea-green *si*.

Black swan's
cor anglais
asserts
amber *la flat*.

∾

I was too late
I was out of time
I was and now
here I am.

Whooper white
with a round
bullseye
of a breast.

My dearest wish and
my greatest ambition:

To be a virtuoso
unmoved by any storm.

But too late—
when my right wing
like a branch lifting heaven
snapped—

My bow wing dangled
from my sorry shoulder.

An octave hides
inside my spine.

An audible shift spanning
a great distance
—a distance I felt
as eternity.

Too late when
I was narrated
to the stage

with only the
required acre of force.

Iron taste
mouth.

Silver shining
ears.

I, alien—

turned
my back
to audience.

    ADAGIO

Swallow enough noise to sunder.

I might be heard.

Outside the human channels of dissonance.

I might be given voice.

Marked by the imperative.

Or what you call fate.

My record of this will be nothing.

Short of translation.

Is it my story that moves you.

Or is it the sight of swans.

Will no one come back for me.

I will be left so unresolved.

The black violin-case starts up.

The telltale rattle of coffins.

The bridge becomes too heavy.

For the burnished body to bear.

Is it the sight of swans?

That lifts in the throat?

Aims to strike the teeth?

Filling a breath?

With some slow spinning Air?

Is this a lament?

An aria discovering Light?

Do clouds tremble on my approach?

Are the formants snowcapped?

The swan's golden cry is blinding

ALLEGRO MA NON TANTO

Quick and bright
the horses
—but not too much.

Look down at the road
disappearing
between a pair of legs.

So the years go
in one brisk movement.

What it would take
for horses to fly.

For now he is spending
obscenely on lobster & champagne.

[Aino pregnant for the third time
warned him he was becoming
strange, unpleasant]

In 1907 he complained
of horses roughing the road
of his voice.

A mentor wrote that
he would soon be dead
unless he stopped
drinking, smoking.

Sibelius himself remarked:
This boozing—in itself an
exceptionally pleasant occupation—
has really gone too far.

[Aino gone away
to the sanatorium]

The specialist who reined in
his horse throat forbade him
to drink for the rest of his days.

He vowed never
to drink again.
And for seven years indeed
he did not.

[According to Aino
the happiest period
of their marriage]

But as the saying goes
you can lead a horse
to water but you can't
keep him from
drink.

When the war began
Sibelius galloped into debt
and cut off his grizzled mane.

There was a growing tremor
in the hooves. The tremor was essential
to him in the way that fire
is essential to clarity.

With the help of
a fortifying font of wine
whom he called
his most faithful friend
he continued to compose.

[Aino remains
silent]

Heaped in a laundry basket
in the dining room
were many manuscripts.

[Aino leaves
the room]

Among them probably
sketches for his
eighth symphony
which he had completed
many times.

And burned
once.

[Aino could not say
what he gave to the fire]

After the burning
his hands shook
and his eyes clouded over.

Perhaps he drank to still
his trembling hands.

It is said that he said:
All of the doctors who told me
not to drink, smoke
are now themselves dead

—but I go on living.

Silence of Järvenpää

Must empty in order to be rung.
I could give up bathing in cold water.

There are days to empty.
There are days I must.

The oak is cracking the sky black.
Night yolk streaking down the middle.

Inside of some pianos there is a pool.
Plinking into which are my ghost notes.

Winter makes you hungry to eat at the piano.
Fingers slipping on the old grease.

Keys like fat buttersticks.
Like a mouthful of oats like a groan of honey.

Winter makes you unstick the violin.
Coax the drawer from the hinges.

What will fit in the violinlung.
Thoughts in the shape of coins.

Sand in the shape of salt.
Any hour of water.

A bow trembles like a folded wing.
A bough whistles in the iron wind.

A bough is meant to be leaned on.
A bow is a beautiful crutch.

Steadies the cold water nerves.
Tongues of ice elating the trees.

Touching the Verb

Ask me what I'm holding
들다 is the verb I might use

But my mother says
들다 she means lift

As in
The trees lift their great arms
to pull the wind in closer

A group of trees gathers
every apple-shaped prayer we toss up

The tree is about my height
That is
the height I would be
if I were a tree
if I were a tree rooted to live

My mother held me
because she knew the ground
and I had to be kept at a distance

When I hold a purse
a poem or a person
I shake out the inside

This weather holds me
for a moment then it passes

The tree hat dips in the wind pours
its head into mine

Chestnut drops from above
some thoughts are not mine to think

I think the name for a group of trees
is something I could never know

들다 sometimes lets you go
to enter to penetrate
to permeate to saturate

This is how the leaves turn
단풍이 들다 curiously
the leaves are the subject

The leaves look at me
Blood brightens their faces

What they hold is their own
emptiness which burning might fill
The leaves hold

At moon's urging
night's blade draws each tree
out of its skin

The leaves hold that fury until
they have no need
for hands anymore until wind
steals their hands away

Trees what are you
trying to tell me how
are you trying to hold me

Sometimes I'm

1.

Sometimes I'm—I feel
like a man in a red T-shirt
living in the body of a babe.

When was the first time we ever
had a good laugh together?

The feeling of our bare asses
on the new blue couch. No—the sigh
of our single pillow when we were
too broke to keep our heads apart.

2.

Sometimes I'm not
breasts
I'm something
better.

Haven't decided
what yet.
But if I'm
it's a woman's.

She says I'm
like a pillow princess
but for everything.
I'm not!

I'm like myself only
I'm in the difference

When she changes her mind
I'm selling Asian pears
slicing them up all the juices
making a little pool in my palms.

I'm exhausted I'm
dripping I'm
euphoric

I'm too large
to be held.
I'm the movement
being born into.

3.

Yes is I enough to be!
Yes is I have no more reasons not to.

I leave my apartment
I go into women
I'm dancing in the women
I always have the right shoes.

I'm up to my neck in I'm
and I'm beautifully.

Las Calles

History did not interest me
until I could look forward
to my own pastness.

I did not know there was a sound
silence made as it laps at the body's shore.
Only that I heard it too late.

Black dusk already curtains my walk.
Tomorrow may be gone.
But there are always new yesterdays.

Today the nations
on the backs of my hands spill
ink from their borders.

I do not have to tell you there is
no exiting your particular unhappiness.
Such a state is walled.

Has edges in time or space.
You understand.
Don't you?

Perhaps you have inhabited the verbs
of *ser* and *estar*
which some strangers often confuse.

Spanish distinguishes between two ways of being.
One that fluctuates.
Another you cannot escape.

A kind local let me know
I did not inhere in Cuba but was only here
until I met the border of my stay.

Could she exit through the verb?
O eres en Cuba?
She laughed but did not correct me.

Ser y estar are each roads
to a different kind of oblivion.
Though of course this is all relative

to the subject travelling on these roads.
What about death?
Yo estoy muerto.

For I was once alive.
Who can say that they have prepared
their body for old age?

That they did not turn
from one oblivion to chase
another? Of course this is a sure road

to death. The joints go first.
Grating the limbs hard enough to burn.
No one can dance forever.

Skin draws back like a shoreline.
Enamel oceans of ash.
The spine unhooks itself from the column.

PLAZA DE LA CATEDRAL

It is a square that encloses
the Catedral de San Cristóbal
which once enclosed the remains of a body

which I am told once belonged
to Christopher Columbus.
Though who is to say whether that body

still encloses him. *¡O restos e imagen*
del gran Colón! Mil siglos durad mudos
en la urna. Al Código santo de nuestra nación.

He had requested to be enclosed
in Santo Domingo
La Ciudad Colonial

but not even saints get to choose
where they lie, Cristóbal—
for when France seized Hispaniola

he was laid back to rest
in La Habana and when Cuba seized
its own self back

he returned at last
after some three hundred years
to Spain. What remains

of those who were
killed? They were called
the Taíno

which I have seen
translated as "men
of the good."

The least they should have is his
body. The least they should have
is his blood.

VIA FLAMINIA

The roads of *ser* and *estar* began in Latin:
stare and *esse*. There stands a city
rather than there is one.

Roman cities did not stand still.
They rose slowly as their roads were paved
over and over.

For the most part these roads went straight
without yielding to the urgent press
of the earth.

See where they clasp each other.
This too is a kind of dance.
The roads lead. No choice but to follow.

The rising roads of Rome still entangle the world.
The secret to their longevity I think
is in their concrete, which stands deceptively still.

The oldest surviving written work on architecture
Vitruvius's *De Architectura*
remembers to use volcanic ash from Pozzuoli.

Combined with water and quicklime
it produced a mortar so stubborn it would not settle
the gaps in the aggregate.

The lime clasts in the aggregate, white shards
broken off the worldteeth, were how
the concrete repaired itself.

Between one dancer and another
it is a crack where their hands meet
for two dancers are a whole.

Water enters the cracks and wakes the clasts.
That flesh forms again
plain as an ache.

PASEO DEL PRADO

The expression *dar un paseo* is understood
in English as *to take a walk*. *Dar*
—to give. You give and I take.

No question of who between us has walked
the greater distance.
In 1925 French landscape architect

Jean-Claude Nicolas Forestier traced
the promenade with trees, later
adding marble benches and lions

of cannon-bronze.
I am staying in Hotel Sevilla
with a cacophony of American tourists.

They do not mind that I have joined
their walking tour. One among them
is a salsa instructor from New York

who walks with an absolutely
economical number of steps.
His hands float not at his sides

but in front of his body as though
he is feeling his way through some darkness.
I always say to my students

he whispers to me conspiratorially
if you can walk
you can dance!

Indeed his walk so excites
the eye it seems to transform
the very ground beneath him

into a sleek bewilder of ice.
With such a pair of feet
he could have become nothing

but a dancer, this is true.
But walking is one thing.
A dancer must know how to count.

For in a measure of eight beats
only six steps are ventured: one, two,
three, pause; five, six, seven, pause.

What should we call this silence?
It goes unmarked in our song of
quick, quick, slow; quick,

quick, slow. Silence lies
like a road between these
two states: quick and slow.

I watch the tour disappear into
Parque Central. In the end
his feet will forget themselves.

CALLE EMPEDRADO

In order to pull a body together
you must first know how they come apart.
That is why I have come to La Habana Vieja.

What strikes many tourists looking at this country
for the first time is a downward question.
Where does this go.

A country that does not move
but has been captured.
A colony of wrong time.

After the 1959 revolution
the trade embargo stopped
the importing of steel

which was used for reinforced
concrete. They had to make do with
stone, cement, bricks.

The architect Ricardo Porro
found another way when he devised
those sloping brick domes

for the Cuban Ballet School.
They curve so sensuously I cannot help
but reach my hand out

to their faraway flesh.
The dance school was abandoned
before its completion. It is empty inside.

CALLE ZULUETA

It is said that only with great
slowness is it possible to amend
the poor layout of the streets.

Cobbled with the bald heads of the Chinese
holding their breath in the great downpour
of the rainy season. Step lightly.

Humboldt, too, travelling through the Americas,
complained in his time about
el mal trazado de las calles habaneras.

Trazado can be translated as *layout*
or *outline* but some speakers will mean
tracing.

A hand must have made these tracings.
A tracing does not inhere.
Can be lifted or brushed away.

El mal trazado. Why does this persist in me?
Another question:
But what am I a bad tracing of?

Oh, the irony of Europeans lamenting
el mal trazado de las calles habaneras
when it is their hands that traced them.

La traza was the foundational pattern
on which Spanish colonial cities were built.
Square hearts pumping roads out at right angles.

It is said that this tracing was impeded
only by geography. As if the colony might be peeled
from the island like a memory.

Where does this go.
Another question:
Who will go with it.

As if tongues can flatly
resign. As if faces can wake
out of a mask.

CALLE DE LOS MERCADERES

Spanish colonials aspired to make landscape
legible. Can it be said that this is the aim
of all architecture?

It is difficult to read the old tracings
without making footnotes.
In rapid clipped Spanish I ask

for a sentence that will lead me
to Calle Obrapía.
I have been thinking of the street crying.

Wrote Alejo Carpentier: *En todos los tiempos
fue la calle cubana bulliciosa y parlera.*
No material trace is left of these *pregones*.

Except, it could be said,
in the streets themselves.
Calls which were always heard

but escaped unrecorded.
A *pregonero* makes a strong orator.
Figselling divulges an ominous song.

Peanuts in a little bag are calling you.
*Cuando la calle sola está
casera de mi corazón…*

Watch me, dear housewife.
Quick, quick, slow.
Sway of gentle palm trunks.

Slow, slow hips.
The street meets me where I step.
Presses back before I fall.

No pretending legibility
did not mean assimilation.
The street makes a home of your heart.

CALLE OBRAPÍA

It was named for La Casa de la Obrapía
a colonial mansion built in 1665.
Intended to house helpless

orphaned girls it was called
Obrapía for it was a pious work.
The girls chosen by the patron

were not to have
the blood of a bad race no
they had to be old Christians.

There are two floors.
Interior patio with lots of vegetation.
Stone columns.

Málaga floor tiles.
In 1793 a Baroque portico was added.
Door carved in Spain.

In *De Architectura* Vitruvius famously named
a triad of characteristics for architecture
utility strength and beauty.

Trees for example succeed in all three.
Churches in all but utility.
The human body is only beautiful.

I return to the interior patio.
Are these the columns Carpentier thought
were not merely pitchforks of the conquerors

but rather graced shaded patios,
were garnished by vegetation,
the trunk of the palm tree

enfleshed with the Doric column?
It is possible that the intimate refinement
he wrote about was but a trace of his time.

La Habana that stands around me is one
Carpentier would have found hard to believe.
Columns after all are only bodies

long in space but not time.
I column the city.
I column the faltering streets.

Perhaps the only sort of form that lasts
is that which goes unnoticed.
A trace.

CALLE OBISPO

The bar is called El Floridita.
Hemingway sits at the end of the bar.
The sun must be getting to him.

He harshes a beautiful bronze.
I wish they would cover him up.
I can feel his stare from across the bar.

It is easy to move when the music demands it.
The streets are waking out of belief.
The man behind me is a sudden column.

I stop.
Too many daiquiris.
He stares.

The man's sullen Cuban girlfriend stands apart.
He is from New Jersey.
Though I do not remember asking.

I try not to look at his face.
I saw you dancing he says.
I am standing still.

Tú eres mala!
Todo el mundo te quiere.
You know what happens next.

If the whole world's desire
runs me like a road.
I will not follow.

My heart is running out of the square.
Quick steps over the badly traced.
Quick steps towards or away from the body.

His girlfriend is bored.
She will not meet my pleading eyes.
It occurs to me I must consider.

Whether she could hold me still.
Whether she would.
I can feel the trace of her hands.

Outside the city is still the city.
Roads reassure.
The city is still.

My heart's feet are quick,
quick, slow. The street meets
me with its answer.

It is only after I have returned
that it occurs to me: perhaps
she needed his American citizenship.

I think of her often.
Exchanging one violence for another.
An old kind of currency.

VIA SACRA

Yet it was granted to us
this walking on our own two legs.
It is not so hard to believe

on the Sacred Street
that gods once walked
in this city.

Why write a founding myth?
Why dance to an old song
made anew?

The ancient Romans deified
their dead emperors in a rite
called apotheosis. Death-masked

a body comes down from Palatine
hill along the Via Sacra
to be shown in the Forum.

Then onwards through the city
to Campus Martius to rest
in an elaborate pyre of riches

whose eagle-winged fumes
propel the emperor's soul
all the way up to heaven.

Let me get to the point.
Why do we want to live
forever? Why do I believe

that you will try to remember
me? I am not asking to be
made a god, only that

the living do not leave me
behind. All I ask is that someone trace
my fugitive footprints.

EL MALECÓN

I have lived in the manner of a dance
a contratiempo which is to say
against the time but with

the music. I lived
believing in history
like it is a road that becomes

easier and easier
to walk, a road upon which
the only mode of travel is

faster, or further, only for
my own two legs
to give

my body back to the ground.
So let us walk together,
foreheads streaked

with bonedust
—let us entrust our hearts
into the hands of those

dead, beloved.
How long has it been?
How long will we be?

The sea steps closer.
The sea steps closer.

Seascape Suite

1.

Applause fills the hall as
An ocean would: slabs of it
Licking over us tuned
To the frequency of decay.
I would float but for my feet
Two dull anchors astounding
The seabed. If I extended my
Speech to you that wasted
Limb still hinged on the body
Would you keep my head
Above the surface? Leave me
Below and let me be silent
So that I can hear you
Breathing. Let me forsake
The orchestra and its frailty.
Loosen the bow and let it
Clatter to the stage. Untangle
From the horn stand it mutely
On its softly shining bell. A concert
Is performed with the admission
That it will never sound
Again. A concert is already
Curtained for each note draws
Its own watery veil. A concert
Dies. Are you listening? Your
Every breath is already slipping
Away.

II.

Human ears are not meant for water
        but we believed it was
                a silent world anyway
If water's iridescence is language
        I wish it would refract
                in full sentences
In water's density sound travels
        five times faster than in air
                reaches further than light
Where even light is afraid to go
        whose voices persist
                in the frigid blackness
Spring will never come silently
        but instead brims with
                entropic noise
In light's absence arises
        a language to sound out
                the colour of the future past
How many ways of looking at
        air? Only as many as
                what bodies draw it in
The human body too is
        permeable
                —susceptible
Water's density makes sonic
        inscription possible
                —fatal.

III.

The wind crumples the waves like a sheet.

Ice cracks whitely off the shelf spit-shined and blinding.

Weddell seals moon their sweet blue crooning.

The right whale bays its huge brassy brays.

Humpback hums the old songs into new.

The wind crumples the waves like a [FOGHORN]

Ice cracks whitely off the shelf [FLAILING THROUGH THE AIR] and blinding.

Cleaner [THE OCEAN A VESSEL] shrimp calls its customers with its claps.

Clownfish chatter [OCEAN FULL OF] their teeth [VESSELS] clacking their jaws.

Weddell seals moon [WANDERING THE FOG] their sweet blue crooning.

The right [CLANGING STEEL PILES] whale bays its huge brassy brays.

Humpback hums the old [INTO THE SEAFLOOR] songs into new.

The wind crumples [AIR GUN BLAST

    BANG

    BURST

    BLARE

    BOOM]

The right whale bays its huge [TRAWL SCRAPING ALONG]

Clownfish [CARGO SHIP AT 20 KNOTS] clacking [PROPELLER CAVITATING]

Ice cracks [DRILLING RIG] AND [ENDLESS WHIRRING]

[OCEAN VESSELS WANDERING] their sweet blue [FOG]

[CLANGING STEEL PILES] songs [INTO THE SEAFLOOR]

[FOGHORN FLAILING THROUGH THE AIR] [VESSELS WANDERING THE FOG]

[AIR GUN BLAST [AIR GUN BANG [AIR GUN BURST [AIR GUN BLARE [AIR GUN

[

IV.

If [   ] in the sea
and no human can hear it
does it [   ]?

If [   ]
and no [
                    ]?

If [

                    ]?

[

                    ]?

V.

What now are we applauding for?

Ode

Hulled
like a boat.

Saluting me
adrift in audience

raising your trim
black sail.

I could mistake you
for a horse

galloping
motionless

on your three
black legs.

Or perhaps
a shaded pool

forest-deep
and brimming

from which
I lift my head

chin dripping
black silt.

Not in prayer
but out

of obedience
I knelt

with only
two tremors

for hands.
I called you

O god of stillness
O lidded vault of thunder

O faultless mirror
O black slap of lacquer

O slick ivory spine
O won't you turn

O my body unbound
O into song

Emergency Orchestra

The trees want
me to recite.
What do you save

from the disaster? Hunting
rifle, camera, cast
-iron pan. The Buddha

wants nothing. He is
only a porcelain
statue. What do you say

in the disaster?
I want
to untangle the voices

of past from those
of present. I want
to recover

the last point in
history at which
we could have turned

around. The voices
are living and they
want

to go somewhere.
I want to let them.
I want

the violins to shimmer
I want them to stand
for impermanence

while the soloist
hangs over them
like an omen

—you too
will one day find
yourself alone

Portrait of Accompanist

Women always need
an answer he says

we cannot ever let anything
sit. But no one answers me.

What bare mother begat the world?
Whose slaughter?

Does he watch me?
Does he turn away?

Who felled the oak?
Who will tend the barley?

Which backwards living?
Whose longing stirs me?

What emerges from the cracked shell of the sky?
Must I keep the borders?

Do I lie?

On Disappointments in Music

It was staggering Sibelius's love
for the violin. Even as day and night
swept around him he felt he could never
practice enough. But one day he woke
to find in place of his violin bow a bitter
stalk of winter. It was time for the lover
to realize his love would never be
enough. Too late too old too full
of tremor. He picked up his pen
and grieved. For what else was there
left to do? He wrote until there were
no more voices inside. One night
he found that the only sound left
inside his body was that of ice
melting. He had had enough.

Aria

A slow, honeyed appetite. Cheap scotch. The way you
talk to yourself soaring and yellow as you come up
the stairs and I know it's you. You surprising me
with the cheap scotch in your bag. Your little bag tossed
on a chair, clinking. One bag for each of us. The sunlit
orchard and your insistence on biting into every kind
of apple, leaving a trail of them as you go. The sun
gazing right at you. You winking back, with both
eyes. You telling me you don't bite, and then biting.
Being bitten. White sandflesh that soon blushes brown.
Your mouth's impossible stretch as if waking from
a great sleep. The first note, wavering. The operas
of Mozart and also Bizet. The sound ripening
in the crown. Startling round luminous shivers. One
more song. Another still. The tongue a loosened
root. Hair shaken free from the branches like moon
curtains. The dress you'll be buried in, the coat I won't
grow into. The company of trees. The trees learning
our voices, already wind. The sensation of wind. Your
breath on me in the morning, uncurling me awake.

Yellow

All around us are yellow things
—like when I come through
the door and you peel the stubborn
weather from my cold blue face.
Or when my rough skin smells
like your smooth skin as though
we were fried in the same oil.
Yellow, like when we were a pair
of wriggling fish hauled up
in the same net—our backs unsettled
by sunlight. Or was it when I seized
a fistful of your cotton nightshirt,
when no part of me but the hands,
hardened, heavy, heedless with hunger
—when only my hands remembered
what colour was. Oh, childhood?
That warm & weatherless room
from which you are missing—it was once
yellow, too.

Modality

When I met you I could have been
a believable boy. What was my name
for myself before strangers

called out *chinois*? I had nothing
to say except for
what couldn't be heard

anyway. Nothing against *le chinois*
but that I could have become
him. Could speech then

have shed the husk
of my voice? Could it be
that I was illegible, that

not even English
would save me here?
At the symphony your dress

might have flowered
and moved like skin. What wasn't I
wearing when the usher caught me

entering the women's
bathroom? He might have said
C'est pour les femmes.

You might have poured
your words right back.
Could I say

what happened next, in this
or any language? I'm certain
only that I had to pee and

so I did. At Lionel-Groulx
there could have been a man
who followed us to argue

with you, who threatened
to beat *ton chum* up
once we left the station.

What violence was made
possible in that language
I couldn't recognize

myself in? Could it have been me
he was threatening? All this
French talk believing me

a boy. *Quand j'étais.*
J'aurais pu être.
How should I put this—I am.

I am.

Lyric You

Just down the street from
where you are I am sitting at a cafe
believing in you. Thinking of you
has helped me put certain things
in perspective. For instance I wish
for *I* to record only its encounter
with *you*. You are the one who
rehinges all the names: your face
daisies at the sun, you glory
up the bare hill rallying the squirrels,
your voice trucks through the traffic
running reckless down the roads,
you catch the circling snow in your
sleepy lashes. What is my language
really for? Not to languish on the page
unheard & unlived, but to hold another
person, to address them—it's true
none of my poems would matter
if I didn't have the words to reassure,
to cheer, to delight, to soothe, to free
you. To make room for us, for how
we will be present together. I promise
to write to you through disaster, in
the face of violences sudden & slow
—I promise to never let you go.

Emergency Orchestra

To end without resolution.

To leave a hole for unending time.

To believe that time faces only one direction.

To live as though there is enough of it.

To carry on forever.

Argument

If I was once a small
    world having begun again
        Then what should I call this body
        I once believed was mine

If I pretend I owe nothing
    to being which gave me everything
        Then this world is a mother
        from whom I have turned away

If mothers do not dream of anything
    but the disasters you are to inherit
        Then my every future self is always
        turning back toward

If our word for world is rooted
    in *weoruld* meaning Age of Man
        Then I want a way to speak
        of the worlds before our time and after

If the body must bear
    the marks of its past
        Then the body will become more
        than what it knows

If we do not forget but rather
    fail to attend
        Then call memory up
        for she is lonely in the house of your heart

If you trace my face and come away
    with fingers streaked with dusk

If *I* records nothing
    but another fraught edge

If sound is effervescent
    and the song lost to time

If my arms
    if your world

If mothers
    if memory

And if we are still strangers
    if I never really reach you

    Then let's climb into bed together
and wake with gentler faces

    Then let speech forsake me
and flock softly to *you*

    Then let me listen to what I can
never hold that brief and utter beauty

    Then a kept promise
then again tomorrow

    Then daughters
then fugue

    Then I will stretch my voice out
to you anyway

NOTES

The "Emergency Orchestra" series draws on *The Composer's Advocate* by Erich Leinsdorf.

"I, the poet, the euphemist" responds to the increase in anti-Aisian volence in 2020.

The series "Portrait of Sibelius" includes details about the life of Jean Sibelius from Erik Tawaststjerna's biography, *Sibelius*. The "Allegro moderato" also draws on motifs from the Finnish national epic, the Kalevala, which inspired much of Sibelius's work.

The recording referenced in "From Which Time" is that of Jascha Heifetz with Sir Thomas Beecham conducting the London Philharmonic.

The punctum mentioned in "Camera" is one of two concepts developed in Barthes' *Camera Lucida*.

The title "Silence of Järvenpää" refers to the period of Sibelius's life during which he produced no major works, retreating to his countryside home to work on his eighth symphony.

"Las Calles" references Alejo Carpentier's essay "La ciudad de las columnas." The lines "O restos e imagen…" are from Christopher Columbus's epitaph while his remains were in the Catedral de San Cristóbal.

"On Disappointments in Music" borrows its title from Anne Carson's short talk of the same name.

ACKNOWLEDGEMENTS

"Touching the Verb" first appeared in *Vallum Magazine* as a winner in the 2023 *Vallum* Poetry Award.

"Sometimes I'm" and "Aria" originally appeared in *The Ex-Puritan*.

"Lyric You" was first published in *The Walrus*.

"Yellow" first appeared in *Maisonneuve*.

The "Emergency Orchestra" series originally appeared in *Concordia University Magazine*.

"Portrait of IIIIIIIII" was first published in *Gulf Coast*.

Thank you to the team at Véhicule Press, and thank you, David Drummond, for the amazing cover!

Thank you, Michael Prior, for seeing something in my work when all I had was a single poem of unwieldy length. Thank you for seeing a book when I didn't know I had one.

Thank you to the creative writing community at Concordia! Thank you, Liz Howard, for your generosity and honesty. I'm so grateful to have been able to work with you. Thank you, Sina Queyras, for always telling me what I need to hear, for seeing the work I was trying to do. Your workshop opened my eyes to what poetry can do and how it resides in the body. Thank you, Gillian Sze, for your kind words and encouragement. I'm glad I took your advice. Thank you, Stephanie Bolster, for finding that fierce and fearless self. Thank you for all your care, for helping me cultivate that care for these poems. Thank you, Alexandra Pasian, for getting me started, for introducing me to the poets who would become my contemporaries. Thank you, Sarah Burgoyne, for your close and attentive listening. Thank you, Prathna Lor, for your thinking, for your questions.

Thank you, Montreal, for your community. Thank you to all the poets and writers who have met me for coffee, whom I've met at readings and panels and signings, whose writing and thinking continues to keep me company, and I hope I will see you soon.

Thank you to my family. And thank you, Isabela Marino, for loving this book before it ever took form.

Signal EDITIONS

MICHAEL PRIOR, EDITOR
MICHAEL HARRIS, FOUNDING EDITOR

Robert Allen • James Arthur • John Asfour, trans.
John Barton • Doug Beardsley • Paul Bélanger
Linda Besner • Walid Bitar • Marie-Claire Blais
Yves Boisvert • Jenny Boychuk • Asa Boxer • Susan Briscoe
René Brisebois, trans. • Mark Callanan • Chad Campbell
Edward Carson • Arthur Clark • Yoyo Comay
Don Coles • Vincent Colistro • Jan Conn • Geoffrey Cook
Lissa Cowan, trans. • Judith Cowan, trans. • Mary Dalton
Ann Diamond • George Ellenbogen • Louise Fabiani
Joe Fiorito • Bill Furey • Michel Garneau • Susan Glickman
Gérald Godin • Lorna Goodison • Richard Greene
Jason Guriel • Michael Harris • Carla Hartsfield
Elisabeth Harvor • Bridget Huh • Charlotte Hussey
Dean Irvine, ed. • Jim Johnstone • D.G. Jones
Francis R. Jones, trans. • Virginia Konchan • Anita Lahey
Kateri Lanthier • R. P. LaRose • Ross Leckie
Erik Lindner • Michael Lista Laura Lush
Errol MacDonald • Brent MacLaine
Muhammad al-Maghut • Nyla Matuk • Robert McGee
Sadiqa de Meijer • Robert Melançon • Robert Moore
Pierre Morency • Pierre Nepveu • Eric Ormsby
Elise Partridge • Christopher Patton • James Pollock
Michael Prior • Medrie Purdham • John Reibetanz
Peter Richardson • Robin Richardson • Laura Ritland

Talya Rubin • Richard Sanger • Stephen Scobie
Peter Dale Scott • Deena Kara Shaffer
Carmine Starnino • Andrew Steinmetz • David Solway
Ricardo Sternberg • Shannon Stewart
Philip Stratford, trans. • Matthew Sweeney
Harry Thurston • Rhea Tregebov • Alice Turski
Peter Van Toorn • Patrick Warner • Derek Webster
Anne Wilkinson • Donald Winkler, trans.
Shoshanna Wingate • Christopher Wiseman
Catriona Wright • Terence Young